Blinded by Love
Saved by Grace

Blinded by Love Saved by Grace

Selena Spurlock

CHARIS GRACE PUBLISHING

Blinded by Love, Saved by Grace

Copyright © 2024 by Selena Spurlock
All rights reserved.

Scripture quotations marked (KJV) are scripture quotations from The Authorized (King James) Version. Rights in the Authorized Version in the United Kingdom are vested in the Crown. Reproduced by permission of the Crown's patentee, Cambridge University Press

Charis Grace Publishing LLC

charisgracepublishing@gmail.com

Place of publication: Virginia Beach, Virginia

For Global Distribution
Printed in the United States of America

Paperback ISBN: 979-8-218-38375-6
Library of Congress Control Number: 2024906089

Cover Design by: Traci L. Chisholm

Acknowledgements

First, I would like to thank God, who is the head of my life and who has given me strength and the ability to walk with grace.

I would like to thank my family for always being there; My mom and dad, my sister, my niece, and my girls who support me.

I am also grateful to my cousins, who call and check on me and stop by to see if I want to ride out.

I wanted to personally thank my cousin, Shemeka, for always being there to help with anything that I ask of her without hesitation or complaints. I love you and appreciate you more than you know.

I am also thankful to Felicia for just being a friend and listening anytime I needed to vent.

Thank you, Devon, for all the meals and walks to exercise, and chats about life.

Thank you, Tina, for motivating me to move forward, and teaching me to not let my disability define me. . . "Rest in Eternal Peace."

Minister Anderson, thank you for leading me back to Christ.

Pastor Reed, thank you for teaching me God's Word, and leading me to Christ.

Thank you, Minster Payne, for helping me learn self-worth.

I also want to thank the first responders and VCU staff who took great care of me, and the wonderful nurse who took great care of me. She even looked out and bought me Chick-fil-A. I am grateful that she gave me such motivation. I thank you all so much and thank God for all of you. You don't know how much you mean to me; I never got the chance to personally thank you and tell you how special you all are to this gal. I close by thanking God for placing such amazing people like you in my life. I can't thank him and you enough!

I would like to especially thank the students and staff from The Department for the Blind and Visually Impaired, Richmond, Virginia, for showing me that there is life after blindness.

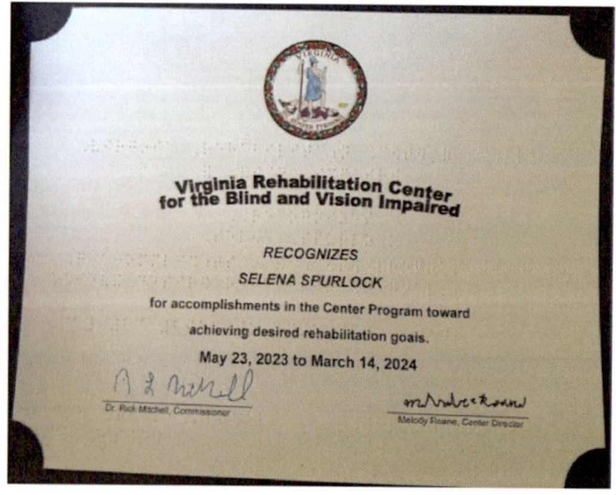

". . . we are more than conquerors through him that loved us" (Romans 8:37).

Contents

Chapter One: Who I Am

WHO AM I ... I'm a mother, I'm a daughter, I'm a queen, but most of all, I am a SURVIVOR! I was raised in King William, Virginia by two adoring parents who married at a young age. I am the middle child of three. I had a brother who died at birth, making me the oldest living. We were raised in a loving home with a very hard-working father who taught me how to be independent, and to never have to rely on a man. He taught me the value of a dollar and how to work hard, while I was young, and put my coins away. A saying that was passed down from his father,

"A fool and his money shall soon part," was somehow burned into my brain from him.

Life as a child couldn't have been any better. Most of my childhood was spent with my grandparents, on their farm, helping them. They had so many different animals. It seemed like they had millions of pigs, goats, cows, chicken, ducks; you name it. There was never a dull moment. Mom would go to BINGO and leave my siblings and I with my grandparents. She would return, and sometimes would come to the room and say, "Y'all come on, let's go." I would reply, "We are sleeping." At times, it would work, and she would let us stay, but other times she would make us go home. We never wanted to

leave. My grandmother was such a sweet lady. She was the rock of our family, the matriarch. Everyone just loved her. She would feed every child that came around. They all took a liking to her, so much so, that she was everyone's, "Grandmama," as they called her. We would go to the bakery and get truckloads of bread and cakes for the animals. We loved the task, as well as all the other kids who came down with us.

I came from a hard-working family. I am familiar with the kind of work that some might be a stranger to. My family and I would be out in the heat, picking greens, potatoes, squash, etc., you name it. What amazed me was that, in the midst of all this hard work we

engaged in, there was still another obstacle that required grit and determination to overcome. My grandfather is completely blind. I often wondered how he could manage a farm without the ability to see! Sometimes I would stare and say to myself, "I wonder if he is completely blind," because he would say, "What are you staring at me for?" Some people would come up to me and say, "I know your grandfather can see." They were so amazed at the things this blind man would do; it was so unbelievable to them.

However, this was not the only obstacle to overcome. Years later, my grandmother became a double amputee, in addition to having a triple heart bypass surgery, from

which she managed to recover. She would still clean the house, wash the dishes, and cook those delicious meals I loved. She was the strongest woman I knew. Our lives were never the same after she passed away in 2014. Not only did she show her love for us, but she also constantly told us that she loved us. Oh, how I miss her cooking, her hugs, love, and most of all, her advice.

There were many more things about my upbringing that has contributed to the fabric of my life thus far. My family was tight-knit, and the men took care of home. However, we had a few cheaters on both sides of the family, and this seemed accepted, like it was the "new normal." It was common to see

married folks bringing their side piece around or family gatherings where the wife was there while the other woman was present. I struggled to understand how something so abnormal could be considered acceptable. I began to question if something deeper was behind this behavior.

During my teenage years, my mother was very strict when it came to boys. In spite of this, my heart rebelled. Every teenager has a childhood crush. There was a tall, light, complicated, bad boy that captured my attention when I was about fifteen. I don't know what it was, but I was head over heels in love. His tall, thin stature, and those big sexy lips gave me cold chills whenever I was

in his presence. I had butterflies whenever I was around him. My cousin and I would talk about the older guy she liked, and I would talk about my teenage love. He was a lot older, so I knew he was like forbidden fruit. Everyone knew that I had a thing for him, and eventually he found out. It would be during one summer cookout, years later, when I realized he noticed me too. He approached me and said, "Only if you were older." He consistently showered me with compliments, and my heart soared. Right then and there I knew he would somehow be a part of my future. Of course, our forbidden connection could not be hidden forever. My parents found out that we were interested in each other, and my father went to look for the

man. The lies surrounding our relationship had my parents thinking we were involved in an inappropriate way. We were attracted to one another, but it was harmless because I was underage. Later we did hookup. By this time, I was grown and had a child of my own. My attraction to a bad boy was not unusual. Most young women find themselves in this position. I loved this man and cared about him as a friend, and always will. We have remained friends to this day.

My freshman year of high school, I met my oldest daughter's father. He was my first sexual encounter. I was so in love with him throughout high school, but there was a lot of dishonesty that clouded our relationship. I

had such a good relationship with his mother, and we still remain close to this day. Right after high school I planned to go to the Navy, but when I took the ASVAB test, I didn't pass. I was planning on retaking it but received news that upended my world; I was pregnant. I had so many mixed emotions. The plan I had for my life had taken an unexpected turn. Months later…. In 1999, my beautiful daughter was born. I was cheated on once again, so I decided to co-parent. My daughter's father and I are still very close friends. He would have been the perfect guy, but we were both very young and really didn't have a clue of what we were doing. We also had a bond that no one could break. He

is another man that I have continued a

friendship with to this day.

Chapter Two:
In Loving Memory of Laela

In 2001, I was in my early twenties when I met this dark-skinned brother. His slow, smooth walk caught my attention while working security for Capital One. I was the type of woman who usually pursued what she wanted, and usually prevailed. I wanted to know more about him, so we conversed for a while and eventually became a couple. He was the perfect gentleman, but his mother didn't like me too well. She was one of those mamas who thought she could choose for her son. In her eyes, no one was good enough for him. She was the true definition of wicked. It

was clear she hated me for some reason. I still don't know to this day why she disliked me, but I was in love with her son, and we were going to be married. In 2003, we found out we were pregnant with baby number two. My first born was not biologically his, but he treated her like his own. This was a very happy time for us, and it finally seemed as though peace had settled into our world. However, further into my pregnancy we received some very upsetting news. The doctor informed us that our baby was diagnosed with tricuspid atresia, a heart defect, and she would have Down Syndrome. The news hit us both like a ton of bricks. The doctor gave us the option to terminate the pregnancy, but this was not acceptable to

either of us. I questioned God and wanted to know what I could have possibly done to deserve this! What quality of life would my baby girl have? I sat down and shared the news with my mother. She said, "Never question God's plans." Those are words I still live by to this day.

On August 5, 2003, Laela Samone was born. She was 4lbs and full-term. I was afraid to look at her, but when I did, she was perfect. There were no physical signs of her having Down Syndrome, but she did have the heart defect that the doctors had detected. The doctors advised that her heart condition could be remedied, but we would have to wait a few months because she needed to

gain some more weight. She was four months when she had her first surgery. I was relieved that the surgery was a success. We were making progress, but this was just one of the three surgeries that she would need. Seeing her lay in a hospital bed with drain tubes, swollen, and the cut that ran from the center of her chest, is a memory that I will never forget. Just seeing my baby like that caused my heart to ache. I never wanted to leave her at the hospital, but I made sure I was there every day. When the time came, she was sent home with an oxygen tank to make sure she was receiving enough oxygen. Considering what she had already gone through, she was a very happy baby who was full of energy. She loved her daddy, her papa, and her sister.

Five months later, surgery two was scheduled on her father's birthday, which is May 19th. On the way to the hospital, I looked back at her with the oxygen tube in her mouth blowing bubbles not realizing this would be one of my final moments with her. We arrived at the hospital, and they eventually came to take her for surgery. She cried looking back at me and my heart fell to the bottom of my stomach. This is the kind of pain that can't be explained; the kind I wouldn't wish on anyone. The surgery lasted most of the day. We kept calling back and they constantly reassured to us that things were fine. At the end of the day, the doctors came out, sat down with us and told us she

did not make it. They took us back to the
room where her lifeless body laid on the
table. I noticed that she had dried up tears in
her eyes. She looked as if she was just
sleeping. I wanted someone to wake me up
from this horrible dream. My baby was gone,
and I couldn't save her. I was angry and lost. I
HAD TO BURY MY CHILD.

At this point in my life, no one could tell me
anything to make me feel better. I felt like a
shell of myself, like I was merely existing, and
not truly living. I think this is where I really
lost who I was... I had no emotions, but I
knew I had to snap out of it for Shalia, my first
born. My relationship with Laela's father
slowly began to deteriorate. We grew further

and further apart. The devastation to us both began to take a toll on our relationship, and her father vanished into thin air. I was confused and lost.

Chapter 3: Forbidden Fruit

As the years past, I started dating and ran into some really interesting guys. Some were crazy, some were just plain not my type, and others were gentlemen but had too much drama.

In the winter of 2006, I was working for a loan company when I was introduced to this tall, dark, handsome guy whom I will just call Dex. One of my coworkers was dating Dex's cousin and thought it was a good idea to play matchmaker. I was sitting at my desk in my office when I looked up and made eye contact with the handsome man who had the biggest

smile. "OH, MY GOODNESS," I thought to myself. I began to finger comb my hair as he walked my way. He came straight into my office and said, "How are you doing?" I replied, "I'm good," but clearly, I was nervous. I thought he was the finest thing that walked planet Earth. He then asked me if he could have my number and I gave it to him. He didn't stay long, and I was glad of that. When he left, I couldn't wait to go out and talk with my coworker the usual "girl talk." I was like, "Girl, he is so fine." I waited for his call, and he finally did call. It was long before things started getting personal.

The first time we were intimate, I became pregnant. I tried to keep this a secret from my

parents because I already had one child. I finally got up the nerve to tell him, and boy he was not happy. He stated that he already had three other children and that he couldn't afford to take care of the baby. He wanted me to terminate my pregnancy, which was not an option for me. I had been secretive about this new guy I was seeing, and when I let the cat out of the bag, I began to hear a lot of negative things about him. However, my parents accepted the fact that they would be having another grandbaby. I was hearing some not so good things about Dex, but I was grown, and I wanted my little family so I got a job and my own apartment, where Dex came to live with us.

My daughter was expected to be born on my birthday, but she was a little stubborn and decided to make her grand entrance three days later, on Sept 25th. She was so perfect and so beautiful. She reminded me of a little Chinese doll. I was so in love. Her father was not present at the time of birth. In fact, he was nowhere to be found. It really didn't bother me at the time because I knew what kind of man I was dealing with. He liked to run the streets. I had started to settle for a lot of foolishness. As years went on, I began to see another side of him. We would argue, and he would call me out of my name. I would just argue back and sometimes hang up the phone. I just wanted that little happy family so desperately, that I stayed and tolerated a

lot of disrespect. Things became worse as time went on. We would attend family cookouts and we seemed like the perfect little family, but as I sat and watched him drink, I knew what type of night I was going to have, especially when liquor was involved.

He would accuse me of the craziest things. Sometimes it happened in front of people, but the worst treatment occurred behind closed doors. We had some great times, and I loved this man with all my heart, but things were not what they seemed. The cycle of putting him out and taking him back was ridiculous. I went out to a gentlemen's club for my birthday one year, and he was fine with it until I got back home. He was furious

and started accusing me of having relations with a stripper. He tried to pull my pants down and smell my privates. This was one of the many crazy incidents that I went through.

One of those drunken nights, I told him not to come to my house, because I, once again, didn't want to deal with the fussing and fighting. My youngest daughter was home and I tried to avoid the mess. He said, "I'm on the way." I grabbed my baby from the bed and hopped in my car, not knowing where I was going. As I pulled out, I saw him in the car that he was driving and, of course, he tried to run me down. I headed towards the city hoping he wouldn't follow me that far. I was shaking and scared for my life. I noticed that

he turned around and didn't continue to follow me. The next morning, I was nervous about going back home. When I finally arrived, my door was kicked off the hinges and every light was on in the house. I didn't call the police this time... I know... crazy right?

Another night, something similar occurred. We argued and my daughter walked in to find her dad on top of me. I told her that we were just playing. She finally fell asleep, and the torment continued. Dex was clearly on something other than liquor and beer. He threatened to kill himself and decided to grab my gun from the drawer and put it to his head.

In fear of what he was capable of, I called my friend, and she heard all the commotion. He insisted that I hang the phone up... so I did. I turned my head so I wouldn't witness him taking his own life. A shot was fired, and I was scared to turn around. When I finally turned, I noticed him still standing, but there was a hole in the ceiling. I tried to get my baby girl and leave. Dex and I started to tussle. He spit in my face and hit me with a beer bottle. When I finally made it out of the house, I headed for the truck and he tried to throw another bottle at me, instead it dented my truck. This time around I decided to call the authorities. They came, took pictures, and charges were filed.

Dex served a year in jail, and I thought this was my chance to escape. A protective order was issued, for which he had no regard. This man had the gift of gab. His sweet words of, "I'm sorry, and I promise this will never happen again," somehow convinced me to take him back once again. I sit and think back now, trying to understand why I was so vulnerable and weak-minded when it came to this man. Dex came home a year later and was the perfect family guy for a while. However, it was all a front. He started exhibiting the same behavior again. He began disappearing for days at a time. Meanwhile, I stopped showing all the love I once showed because I thought he was being unfaithful. He pulled up one morning after being gone for

days and started to cry. He admitted he had a drug problem. I told him that I loved him, but he could not come back home until he got some kind of help.

The next day, I received a call from his sister, telling me he had been rushed to the hospital for chest pains. While he was in the hospital, I ended up speaking with him briefly, but standing firm on my word. I told him that I was not coming to the hospital and he was not welcome back until he got the help he needed. He eventually checked himself into a drug program. Things improved after this, and we had some good times.

However, as time went on, things were back to square one. He began to hang out with certain guys who were a bad influence, once again. Some days were okay, while other days were not. 90% of the time, his family understood the situation and sided with me. His sister would always say, "He has met his match." However, truth be told, I had to learn how to defend myself in those situations. I determined that I would no longer sit and take the abuse. I wanted him to think I wasn't scared, but deep down I was. I thought, perhaps, if I defended myself, the nightmare would end. I kept on doing what I had to do for my children, but I was no longer in love with the man I had been in love with for the past fourteen years. I was constantly

trying to figure out who I was, and had lost myself in the midst of the changes that had taken place over time. I really loved this man and wanted the best for him. He had lots of potential, but was stuck in the past and his old ways. I felt as though I did not give a darn about myself and would look in the mirror and ask myself why I put up with this mess. I realized the why, and it struck me with a force I was not prepared for. I was lost! I had lost focus of what was truly important. I questioned my predicament afresh, asking, "Who is this woman looking back at me?" I no longer wanted to be lost, scared, and confused. I wanted to feel the beauty again that everyone else could see. Behind the beauty was a lost soul who wanted to be

loved so badly, she had mistaken what real love was. It was time for me to find myself. I found the courage to tell Dex that I was no longer in love with him and that he needed to start looking for a place to live. The look he gave me, told me that he knew I was physically present, but mentally and emotionally gone.

He did not take the news well. We had a few words, and then, things took a more serious turn. He grabbed his shotgun from the laundry room and cocked it. I did not show any fear, but I was trembling inside. Shortly after that, he left and decided to go and sit in his truck. I guessed he was trying to cool the heat of his anger off. As I sat in deep thought,

it dawned on me that the man would probably end up killing me or disfiguring me for life. I had the sinking feeling that I would not leave the relationship unharmed. He had threatened to kill me or "make it so that no one else wanted me." Our relationship was beyond repair, and I was drained. He did not want to work. All he wanted to do was hang out with the so-called friends that gave him drugs. I felt so unloved, alone, used, and abused. I was desperate for a way out.

Despite of all the previous efforts from my friends and family trying to get me to leave, I was finally strong enough. After all of the ripping and running up and down the road, pondering and worrying about what this man

was doing, "Was he cheating? Was he using? How was my night going to end this time?" I tried to stop it all and clearly had no control over anything. I was slowly driving myself insane. This was an unhealthy and toxic cycle that I no longer wanted to be a part of. I wanted so desperately to save him because I loved him and felt deep down that he loved me, too.

Now that I look back, someone other than him needed to be saved also, and that someone was me. I felt that all of this was done in vain. I had given one hundred percent of me to this man, and in return, I had to end up fighting to save my own life. All the prayers I requested for God to answer didn't

go unnoticed and were revealed each time, but we tend to at times overlook them.

Weeks later, he left to go hunting before the sun came up. We had argued, yet again, and I was sick with Covid-19. I was not in the mood for another one of his foolish and dangerous rants. The hours passed, and nightfall came. He was still out drinking with the guys. I decided to call him, and we got into another heated exchange. When we spoke, he was out of control, cursing and throwing my ex in my face, in front of his buddies, most likely to show off. I decided to get out of bed and meet him to retrieve the plates he had taken off of my truck that was no longer registered, or in operating use. It was clear that he was

intoxicated, and I did not want him driving in

that state.

Shortly after I pulled up to his mother's

house, where he was gathered with ten of his

buddies, and I approached him. He had a shot

of liquor in his hand, which was more

evidence that he was drunk. "So, we are

doing this tonight?" I asked him to give me

my plates and told him that he could stay

where he was with his buddies. Dex snatched

the plates off the truck and threw them in my

face, leaving a scratch on my nose that

started to bleed. Anger bubbled up inside me,

prompting a reaction. When he walked away,

I hit him in the back of his head with my fist.

He fell to the ground, and I thought for a

moment that it would detour him. To my surprise, he gets up and says, "I'm still going to drive." He almost backed into his cousin's truck and eventually sped down the road, drunk, and without plates on the truck. Only one of his friends made sure I was okay after the ordeal. I made my way home and hurried to lock all the doors. I knew he did not have a key to the top lock for this very reason. His behavior this particular night, was the last straw. I had no desire to deal with him anymore. I had suffered enough embarrassment from him, both in front of his friends, and behind closed doors. I knew if he showed up, he was going to continue to display violent and foolish behavior.

Finally, I laid down in bed, constantly watching my camera and eventually fell asleep. I woke up and my ring camera went off. I watched as Dex backed out and into my parked truck. I texted his sister to come and get him, because I was not going to let him in the house, especially after what had happened earlier that night. I watched from my window as his sister and her boyfriend arrived. They tried to persuade Dex to come with them. He started yelling that he was not going with them. I opened the window at that point and asked them to take Dex with them. He yelled at me and cursed me out. "Freaking female dog, all I care about is my daughter." I told him that I was going to call the cops. "Go ahead and call them, we are going to have a

shootout. Somebody is going to die tonight." I was overwhelmed. I was covid-positive, and all I wanted was some peace in my life. He grabbed the gun from the truck and pointed it at me, while I stood in the window. "I know you did not just point that gun at me!" His sister tried to grab the gun from him, but he was in a rage. His sister's boyfriend tried to intervene at that point and take it from him, but to no avail. They called his cousin, who was close by, and he tried to convince Dex to get into the car, but he refused. I knew Dex was a felon, and I did not want him to go to jail. I also informed them that I was calling the police because the situation was getting out of hand. I dialed the 911 non-emergency line, and placed it on the windowsill, to let Dex

know I was serious. I noticed to my horror, that his sister and her boyfriend were leaving without him. I hurriedly sent a text, begging them not to leave him there.

Then... BOOM... I flew back into my bathroom wall, and all I could hear was a loud ringing in my ears. I stood back, shaken, realizing that I had been shot.

Chapter Four: Surviving the Dark

"You shot me!" I yelled with blood pouring down my face. The pain I felt was unbearable, and at that moment, I did not know if I was going to survive. I prayed to God that He would spare my life, for the sake of my children. Somehow, I knew my eyes were badly damaged. I cried out to God again and asked Him to spare my life, even if I did not have any eyesight. The blood was still running down my face. I remembered that I kept a towel behind my door. I grabbed it and began to wrap my burning face. I remembered that the operator was still on the phone. I told him

that I think I had lost a lot of blood, and

begged someone to come quickly.

At that moment, my thirteen-year-old

daughter came running in, yelling. I told her I

had been shot and asked her to call her sister.

When she called her sister, she answered the

phone. My youngest daughter shouted,

"Daddy shot mama!" The sound of her yelling

in fear is a sound that will haunt me forever. I

stumbled down my stairs and fell at the

entry-way downstairs. I was in severe pain,

yet tried to remain as calm as I could, for my

daughter's sake. I knew that the more

anxious I became, the quicker I would bleed.

Her aunt was still there, so she could assist

us. I slammed the door shut, not knowing if

Dex was still outside with the gun. I sat on the couch, in severe pain, waiting for the paramedics to arrive. The sheriff was the first to arrive on the scene, and I heard him tell the dispatch that my eyes were bulging and that he did not think I could see. That was the least of my worries. My oldest daughter arrived and was all shaken up. I reached for her hand, and she took it. I told her if anything happened to me to take care of her sister.

The ambulance finally arrived and took me down the road to the school football field, where there was a med vac helicopter waiting. They got ready to place me in the helicopter, when I heard my mother asking if

she could ride with me. They did not allow her to accompany me. I was fully conscious, and heard them say that we would arrive in seven minutes. Before I knew it, I heard them announce they were landing on the rooftop and taking me in for surgery. They let my daughter in. "Mom, you're going to be alright," was the last thing I remembered hearing. Soon, needles were being placed... The placement of a tube down my throat filled me with pain I would not wish on anyone.

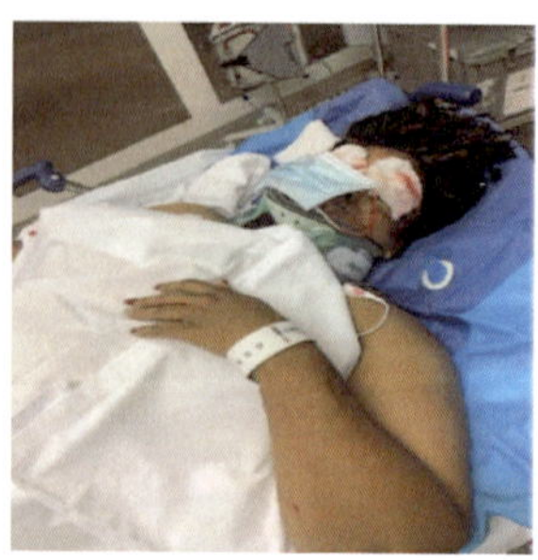

Hours later, I was in a dark place with strange noises. There was something

sticking out of my arm. I tried to pull it out and escape, as if being held hostage. A strange voice sounded in the room and said, "Ms. Spurlock, you cannot pull your IV out." You are in the VCU hospital, in the Intensive Care Unit." I felt my face and it was all bandaged up. My eyes were covered with some sort of eye protector. I was in excruciating pain, and they showed me the button to press for pain medication. This had been the longest two weeks of my life. Since I was Covid-positive, I could not have any visitors.

Weeks went by and I was miserable. I had to try to figure out how to use the phone, so I could at least have communication with the

outside world. I was ready to go home to my children. I broke down and started to cry when the doctor came in. I was told that they were trying to get my blood pressure down before I was released to go home. Not long after he said this, he prayed with me and told me that I could go home that very day. I was ecstatic, yet gave thought to my serious predicament. The shotgun blast to my face had almost taken my life. The pellets broke my nose, shattered my sinus, and some close to the main artery in my brain. They could not be removed. The doctor informed me that if the shot had hit the main artery in my brain, I most likely would not have survived. The shotgun blast had also knocked my eyes out of socket and hit the optic nerve in both. I still

have my eyes, and there are no major deformities in my face. My left eye is a little smaller than the right, and I now live with 12-13 pellets lodged in my face.

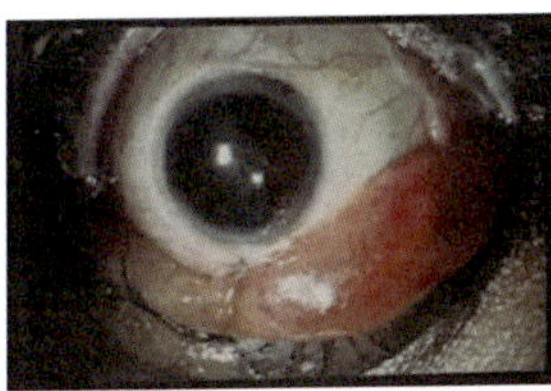 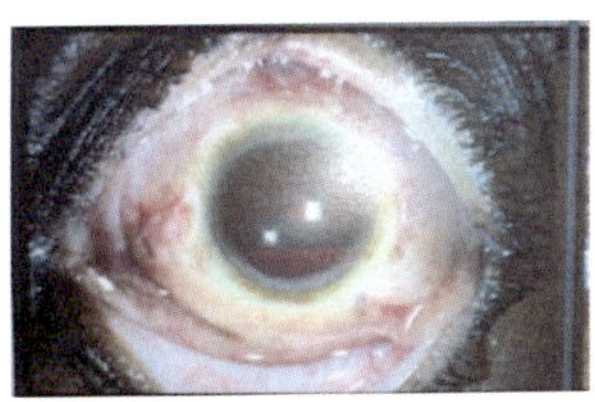

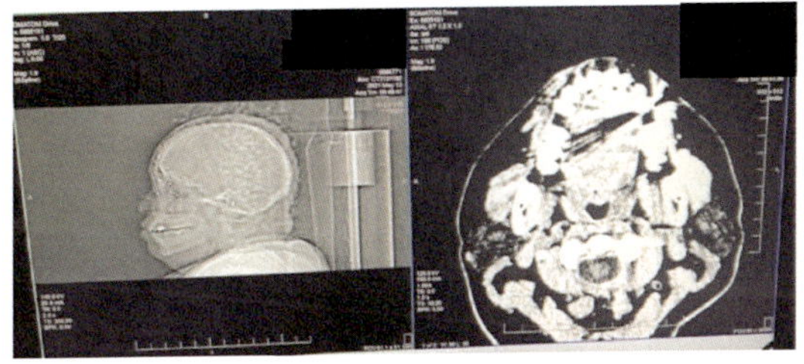

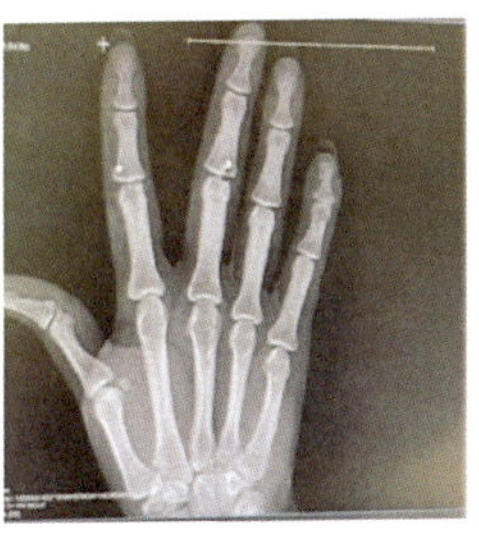

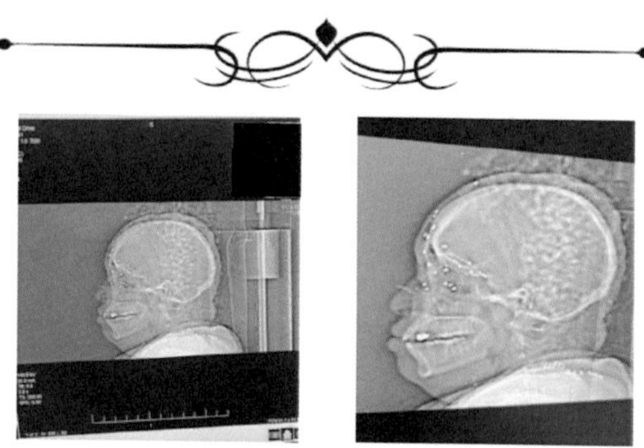

I went home on strong meds that kept me comfortable for a while. Every day, I would wake up hoping to have some sort of sight. I started sleeping a lot, and as I began to heal, depression set in. I questioned many things and even considered taking my own life. I wondered if the quality of my life would be worth it. Walking into walls and falling down my stairs was wearing on me. I hated my life, and I hated Dex for doing this to me. I kept hearing my youngest daughter sit in her room and cry. I knew right then and there I had to snap out of it. I called both of my daughters

and prayed with them. I reassured them that

we were going to get through this.

Dex was charged with aggravated malicious

wounding, but the judge said that the

attorney general could not prove that the

attack was intentional. However, she had

more than enough evidence to prove him

guilty. His charge was dropped down to

unlawful wounding, which broke me down.

Along with the charge of felony, the firearm

gave him five years in prison, along with other

charges. He was sentenced for a total of ten

years, which he was still trying to appeal.

April 2023, I received a call from the

commonwealth attorney with the horrific

news that his appeal was approved. This felt

like a smack in the face to me, because once again, the judge's ruling was incorrect. I am grateful to the attorney general at the supreme court who fought to have the appeal overturned. Months later, I received word that the appeal was revived and denied. I felt a rush of relief that he was denied the ability to come home early. I felt as if I had received some sort of justice.

This case has once again been sent back to the supreme court and was reviewed under a panel of three judges, and the final decision was for him to complete his full sentence. A big thank you to the attorney general in Richmond and the victim witness advocate who supported me through it all. I have given this all to God, and have decided to leave it there. I am committed to focusing on my healing and future.

Chapter Five: Leaning on Faith

My aunt, Minister Anderson, would call to check on me and give me encouraging words. She asked, "Won't you come to church Sunday?" I went and the pastor welcomed me in with open arms. They prayed over me, and I began attending services on a regular basis. God began to reveal a lot to me. I finally began to have a vision without vision. I fasted and stayed in the Word. I was relieved to finally be climbing out of the hole that I was buried in. I started listening to the 700 Club. This brought me to a further breakthrough in my life. One morning, God spoke to me through an episode about a

young woman who was in an abusive relationship. Her boyfriend took a shotgun and shot her in the face, and she laid in the hospital fighting for her life. Her parents came, and the last thing she said to them before she passed away was, "Please forgive him." God wanted me to forgive him. I cried, and, in that moment, I let all of the hate go. I forgave this man for blinding me and almost taking my life.

> *If you ever read this, I forgive you. Life is good and I have been given another chance to get it right and to let others know how good God is; He sits high and looks low. He is always in control.*

They tried to break me down in court with all

the foolish lies, but you can't break anyone

who has been favored by the Lord. Praise

Him, for He is good and knows and sees all.

He is worthy to be praised! Through it all, my

family has been there every step of the way. I

am especially thankful for my daughter

Shalia. I have started school for the blind

where they teach me how to live a normal

life. I am capable of anything everyone else

can do except for driving. I have met some

incredible women who are survivors. My life

coach, who is also a survivor, gave me the

motivation to always love me and stand tall

and proud. She helped me figure out why I

chose to stay. I prayed and asked God to

reveal to me what happened in my past that

made me stay and tolerate the abuse I

endured. He gave me answers, which I

choose not to disclose. I still have days that

are not as good as others, but the good

always outweigh the bad, so I won't

complain.

I just want young women and people who are

visually impaired to know that you can always

rise above difficulties. I want them to know

that anything is possible regardless of their

situation. There are always resources

available. If you need help, don't be afraid to

reach out: 1-800-799-7233. I survived to be

able to tell my story. A lot of women and men

don't have that second chance. Know your

worth and love yourself even if no one else

does. Don't be another statistic. There is always help available. I chose to stay, and I had to learn how to fight back. No one deserves to go through what I have endured. It's just not worth it. If you are in an unsafe relationship, or situation, please leave and do not delay! Talk to someone who can help and get out. Life is limited, so make the best out of it. Leave, and live in peace. The abusive relationship changed my whole life; this would have been avoided if I had just reached out. Through all my struggles, I survived, and they have made me into the person I am today.

All Things Through Christ Who

Strengthens Me

(Philippians 4:13)

Chapter Six: Living Blind

When people think of blindness, they usually think the worst. I am a living testimony to let you know that it's not as bad as it may seem. With the advanced technology we have today, along with training schools and other resources, people can usually live a pretty normal life. Though, there will at times be some trials and tribulations.

> *I have said these things to you, that in me you may have peace. In the world you will have tribulation. But take heart; I have overcome the world"* (John 16:33, ESV).

I have come a very long way from where I started. I am now living a pretty normal life. I use a lot of technology to help me in my everyday living. An example is my mobile device that I use to read mail, currency, colors, can goods, and so much more, you would really be surprised! I also use an app called "Be My Eyes" that just about does it all. I love the AI feature that will describe a person all the way down to the accessories that you are wearing. I also label a lot of things with braille to differentiate what it is that I'm using. I still love fishing, which I have mastered, and I can't forget cooking and keeping my house clean. I have to thank the School for the Blind and Vision Impaired.

The first time I was accepted at the school for the blind I attended for about a week. I was so nervous, frustrated, and just plain irritated with life. I just wanted Dex to feel the things that I had to endure, I wanted him to live the life of blindness. I would get lost and just sit and cry. I couldn't handle being in an unfamiliar environment; I felt like I would never adapt to my new way of living. I had enough. So I called my mother to come pick me up, and I didn't return until a year later when I felt that I was a little more emotionally stable.

When I returned the teachers noticed a spark. I walked with a new walk and I had a new talk. I was ready and I was committed to learn

and nothing was going to stop me. My classes consisted of brail, which I didn't care for and didn't think that I needed to learn it. However, as time went on, I began to pick it up well with a little push from the instructor. He was amazed at my progress.

Then there was cooking, which I had a passion for anyways, so that was a breeze. Mr. T taught me so much; I learned a lot of different techniques to use in the kitchen. Examples include removing meals from the oven without getting burned, different sounds that alerted me that the food was fully cooked, cleaning up broken glasses, sweeping, organization of foods, measuring

ingredients, making dishes from scratch, and so much more.

Keyboarding was frustrating at times, but this was my main focus because I wanted to return to the working field someday. I learned how to copy, paste, bold, and underline. There is a system we call "Jaws," which is a screen reader that allows me to read everything on the screen. I also learned to navigate the web and much more.

During the orientation and mobility class, I learned to use the white cane to navigate, recognize different textures, shore lining, crossing streets, and traveling different terrains. To say the least, I never thought I

would travel three blocks alone non-visual.

This class definitely gave me the courage that

I didn't even know I needed.

I don't want to forget wellness, because this

gave me the extra push on the importance of

diet and exercise. There were days that I

didn't want to participate but did anyway,

and I always felt better afterwards. This life

experience was a challenge, but I prevailed

and completed this journey. Truly this will

always be an unforgettable and life changing

experience.

"Be strong and of a good courage, fear not, nor be afraid of them: for the Lord thy God, he it is that doth go with thee; he will not fail thee, nor forsake thee" (Deuteronomy 31:6, KJV).

Purple Rose

Beautiful, vibrant under the rays of the sun
stood a purple rose, alone. Who was she?

Leaves purple and full of life, mist dripping
from her petals, under the sunlight flowing
down to the ground below.

Reaching her roots, giving her strength to
stand alone. Who was she?

She loved this land so much her roots became
one with it. A thunder cloud appeared and
flooded the ground with pollution-there was
no solution.

She could not move because she had so much
to prove.

Standing alone, lonely and cold, but her tears she could not hold.

Battered and bruised from the force of the rain, facing the brutality of her terrain. Who was she?

Dormant from the abuse, the pain, she was trying to withstand.

She appeared lifeless from the stress, nonexistent in her own flesh.

Persistent to hold on, for better days were near. A new rain came and washed away all of her fear. Finally, that glimpse of hope was here.

She raised from her crouch to embrace the energy that was given, her petals were replenished, vibrant and purple again. Who was she?

Enduring so much thinking there was no way
out, holding on, keeping her faith, and never
giving up saved her. Who was she?

That purple rose was me, and the storm came
and set me free.
By the grace of God, He saved me.

Selena Spurlock

Embracing the Storm

The storm knocked me to my knees, but they
were never broken

With a little fire and determination in my
soul, it left a glimpse of hope, I realized that
in life there has to be balance.

An unhealthy fruit tree cannot bare healthy
fruit, toxic soil will only destroy it.

There is no good without evil, there is no
victory without failure, there is no happy
without sad, there is no darkness without

light; they both cannot co-exist with one
another.

What will you choose?

I look back at my life and sometimes I cry,
sometimes I smile, but I walk away gracefully
because I'm God's child.

Selena Spurlock

Author's Bio

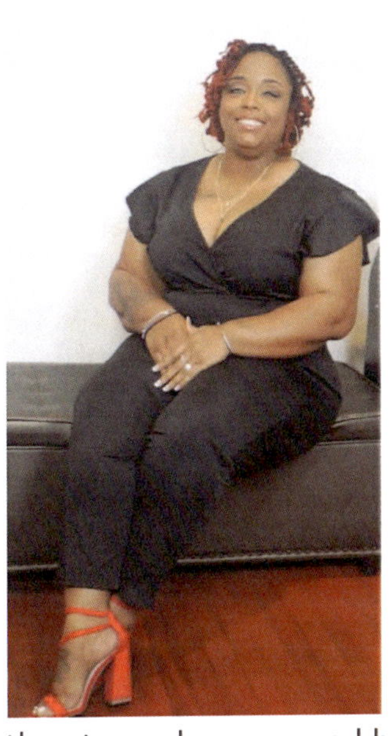

On an uncommonly warm September morning, Selena was born into this world. From the very beginning, she was anything but ordinary. She dreamed big and possessed an indomitable spirit, always illuminating the atmosphere around her. She spent her formative years on her grandparents' farm, residing just outside of Richmond, VA alongside her sister. Her grandparents and parents instilled in her the values of unwavering hard work, unconditional love, and the significance of financial prudence. This upbringing instilled in Selena a profound appreciation for family, and she ultimately created her own, raising three beautiful daughters. Selena is a devoted mother and an exceptionally genuine individual, always willing to lend a helping hand to those in need. Her infectious energy and unwavering optimism draw people in, captivated by her unique and authentic personality. Selena's life took an unexpected turn, veering from the normalcy of her well-established career and family life. In a single, fleeting moment, on a night that evokes longing for the power to alter the course of time, her life was transformed. This night came to be known as The Night of Darkness.

**For woman and men who may be in a
domestic violence situation:**

The choice is yours. Will you continue to live
in fear? Will you continue to walk on
eggshells? Or will you choose to love yourself
and life? Remember, there is always help
available and you're not alone. The **Domestic
Violence Hotline is 1-800-799-7233**; they are
available 24/7!

* 9 7 9 8 2 1 8 3 8 3 7 5 6 *